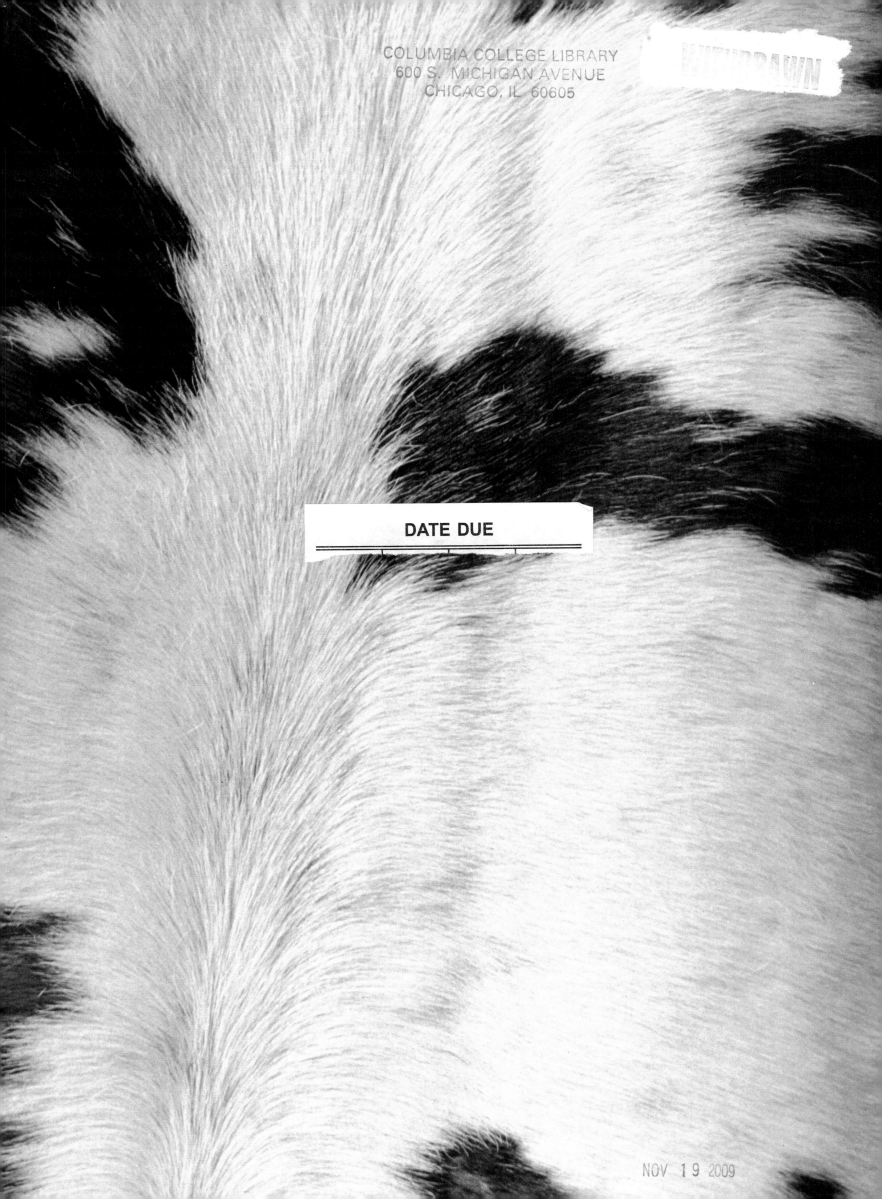

www.bangkokfashioncity.com

SKIN™

BANGKOK FASHION
NOW & TOMORROW
VOLUME.FIVE
www.bkkfashionnow.com

BANGKOK FASHION NOW & TOMORROW
IS A FASHION PUBLICATION SERIES PUBLISHED BY THE
BANGKOK FASHION CITY PROJECT,
UNDER THE **MINISTRY OF INDUSTRY.**
FUNDED BY THE ROYAL THAI GOVERNMENT,
THIS PUBLICATION PROJECT ATTEMPTS TO PROMOTE
THE GLAMOUR OF THAI FASHION BY TOP DESIGNERS
TO A LOCAL AND OVERSEAS AUDIENCE, A CAMPAIGN TO
PROMOTE BANGKOK AS A FASHION CENTRE IN ASIA.

PRODUCED BY **TTIS CO., LTD.,**
THE PUBLICATION COMES IN SIX VOLUMES,
EACH WITH ITS OWN NAME AND THEME UNDER
BANGKOK FASHION NOW & TOMORROW SERIES.
THE VOLUMES, PUBLISHED WITHIN A PERIOD OF 18 MONTHS,
COVER A WIDE RANGE OF FASHION SECTORS FROM:
SCREAM ON HAUTE COUTURE;
STREET ON READY-TO-WEAR;
STONE ON JEWELLERY;
SPUN ON FABRIC BIBLES;
SKIN ON LEATHER FASHION ACCESSORIES; AND
SPEED ON NEW YOUNG DESIGN TALENTS.

VIEWS AND OPINIONS EXPRESSED OR IMPLIED IN
BANGKOK FASHION NOW & TOMORROW
ARE THOSE OF THE AUTHORS OR CONTRIBUTORS.
THEY DO NOT NECESSARILY REFLECT THOSE OF
TTIS CO., LTD. AND/OR THE **BANGKOK FASHION CITY**
PROJECT, UNDER THE MINISTRY OF INDUSTRY.
READERS ARE ENCOURAGED
TO VISIT THE PUBLICATION WEBSITE,
WWW.BKKFASHIONNOW.COM,
AND VIEW THE PUBLICATIONS ONLINE.

FIRST PUBLISHED AND DISTRIBUTED IN 2006
BY **BANGKOK FASHION CITY**
WWW.BANGKOKFASHIONCITY.COM

DEPARTMENT OF INDUSTRIAL PROMOTION,
MINISTRY OF INDUSTRY
6TH FL., RAMA VI RD., RATCHATHEWI,
BANGKOK 10400, THAILAND
T. 662 202 4593/4
F. 662 354 3249
E. INFO@BKKFASHIONNOW.COM

PRINTED AND BOUND IN THAILAND
ISBN 974-94321-8-5

CONTENTS
BANGKOK FASHION NOW & TOMORROW
VOLUME.FIVE

SKIN
KIN CITY

BANGKOK IS A CITY THAT LOVES ITS SKIN.
WHETHER THEY'RE PROTECTING IT FROM THE TROPICAL HEAT WITH THE LATEST UV-SHIELDING CREAM OR SHOWING IT OFF IN DESIGNER CLOTHES AT ONE OF THE CITY'S HIPPEST NIGHTCLUBS, THE DENIZENS OF BANGKOK ARE CONNOISSEURS OF ALL THINGS DERMAL.

IN FACT, IT HAS GONE SO FAR THAT RATHER THAN USING TERMS LIKE THE BIG MANGO OR THE CITY OF ANGELS, PERHAPS BANGKOK SHOULD REALLY BE KNOWN AS SKIN CITY. WHILE PERSONAL CARE AND PERSONAL FLAIR PLAY THEIR PART, IT IS BANGKOK'S LOVE AFFAIR WITH LEATHER THAT IS REALLY DRIVING SKIN CITY'S NEWFOUND PASSION. AS BANGKOK'S FASHION INDUSTRY FLOURISHES LIKE NEVER BEFORE, IT IS ONLY FITTING THAT THE SAME SKILL AND SENSUALITY THAT GOES INTO DESIGNER DRESSES AND CUTTING EDGE STREET WEAR IS FILTERING ITS WAY INTO THAILAND'S LEATHER INDUSTRY.

BUT THE PATH TOWARDS GLOBAL SUCCESS FOR THE INDUSTRY HASN'T ALWAYS BEEN AN EASY ONE. WHILE ALWAYS MOVING FORWARD, THERE HAVE BEEN PLENTY OF POTHOLES AND PITFALLS ALONG THE WAY.

A FEW DECADES BACK, THAILAND WAS KNOWN FOR LOWER-QUALITY LEATHER GOODS THAT WERE OFTEN TIMES KNOCKOFFS OF INTERNATIONAL BRANDS.

FROM THERE, AS THE SKILL OF THAI CRAFTSMEN IMPROVED AND GAINED NOTICE, GLOBAL NAMES SET THEIR SITES ON THAILAND AS A PRODUCTION BASE FOR THEIR ORIGINALS.

BUT NO COUNTRY WANTS TO LINGER BEHIND THE SCENES FOR EVER, AND IT WAS ONLY A MATTER OF TIME BEFORE THAILAND'S LEATHER INDUSTRY, LIKE THE COUNTRY ITSELF, STEPPED UP TO MAKE A NAME FOR ITSELF AS A CENTRE OF SOPHISTICATION AND STYLE.

THESE DAYS, THE COUNTRY'S LEATHER INDUSTRY IS BOOMING, AND AS WELL AS BECOMING A MAJOR PART OF THE LOCAL ECONOMY, IT HAS ALSO MADE A NAME FOR ITSELF ON THE GLOBAL STAGE. AND WITH THE PERFECT MIXTURE OF HIGH-QUALITY MATERIALS, EXOTIC DESIGNS AND AFFORDABILITY, IT IS EASY TO SEE WHY.

AS WITH ANY CREATIVE INDUSTRY OR ART FORM, THE JOURNEY ISN'T COMPLETE, AND THERE ARE COMPETITORS LURKING AT EVERY BEND - IN THIS CASE, ESTABLISHED EUROPEAN MANUFACTURERS AND LOW-COST REGIONAL UPSTARTS -

BUT THAILAND LOOKS TO HAVE LEARNED FROM ITS PAST AND LOOKED TO ITS FUTURE AND IS NOW POISED TO REMAIN A FIXTURE ON THE GLOBAL FASHION SCENE FOR YEARS TO COME.

WHILE THAILAND IS SURE TO CONTINUE COLLABORATING WITH INTERNATIONAL BRANDS AND EXPERTS, THE FUTURE OF THAILAND'S LEATHER INDUSTRY - LIKE ITS FASHION INDUSTRY AS A WHOLE - IS FIRMLY IN THE HANDS OF A NUMBER OF WELL-KNOWN LOCAL FASHION HOUSES AND UP-AND-COMING DESIGNERS.

THANKFULLY, THESE SKILLED HANDS LOOK AS STEADY WITH LEATHER AS THEY HAVE WITH EVERY OTHER PIECE OF THE FASHION PUZZLE.

TOP FASHION HOUSES LIKE GREYHOUND, FLY NOW, ISSUE AND BOUDOIR WILL CONTINUE TO LEAD THE WAY AND GRAB THE HEADLINES,

BUT AN EVEN GREATER NUMBER OF YOUNG DESIGNERS CAN BE FOUND AT UNCONVENTIONAL FASHION HOTSPOTS LIKE JATUJAK MARKET AND SIAM SQUARE WAITING IN THE WINGS, INNOVATING AND WHETTING BANGKOK'S APPETITE FOR BELTS, BAGS, BOOTS AND EVERY OTHER ACCESSORY IMAGINABLE.

WITH THEIR PATH CLEARLY MAPPED AND THEIR IDENTITY WORN ON THEIR SLEEVES, THE FUTURE IS CLEARLY BRIGHT FOR THE DESIGNERS PLYING THEIR TRADE IN THE THAI LEATHER INDUSTRY.

AND IF TIMES GET ROUGH AND THERE ARE MORE BUMPS IN THE ROAD, THEY NEEDN'T WORRY - INSPIRATION IS ALWAYS CLOSE AT HAND IN THIS GLAMOROUS CITY OF SKIN.

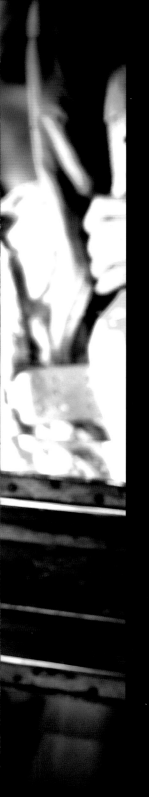

SUPERNATURE

PHOTOGRAPHY. **NAT PRAKOBSANTISUK**
STYLING. **JIRAT SUBPISANKUL**

THEY'RE SOME OF THE MOST FAMOUS NAMES IN THAI FASHION, SO IT'S ONLY FITTING
THAT THEY'VE BRANCHED OUT INTO SATIATING THE DESIRE FOR DESIGNER
ACCESSORIES.

THAILAND'S MOST FASHION-FORWARD BRANDS KNOW THAT IT'S NOT JUST ABOUT CREATING
A LOOK; IT'S ALSO ABOUT COMPLETING IT. FROM BOOTS TO BELTS TO BAGS,
THESE BRANDS ARE DOING JUST THAT - AND DOING IT WITH THE FINESSE AND FLAIR THAT WE HAVE COME TO EXPECT.
SO IF YOU'RE LOOKING FOR SKIN WITH STYLE PLUS THAT SOMETHING EXTRA, LOOK NO FURTHER.

BLOUSE, **FLYNOW**
BAG, **NUCHNA**

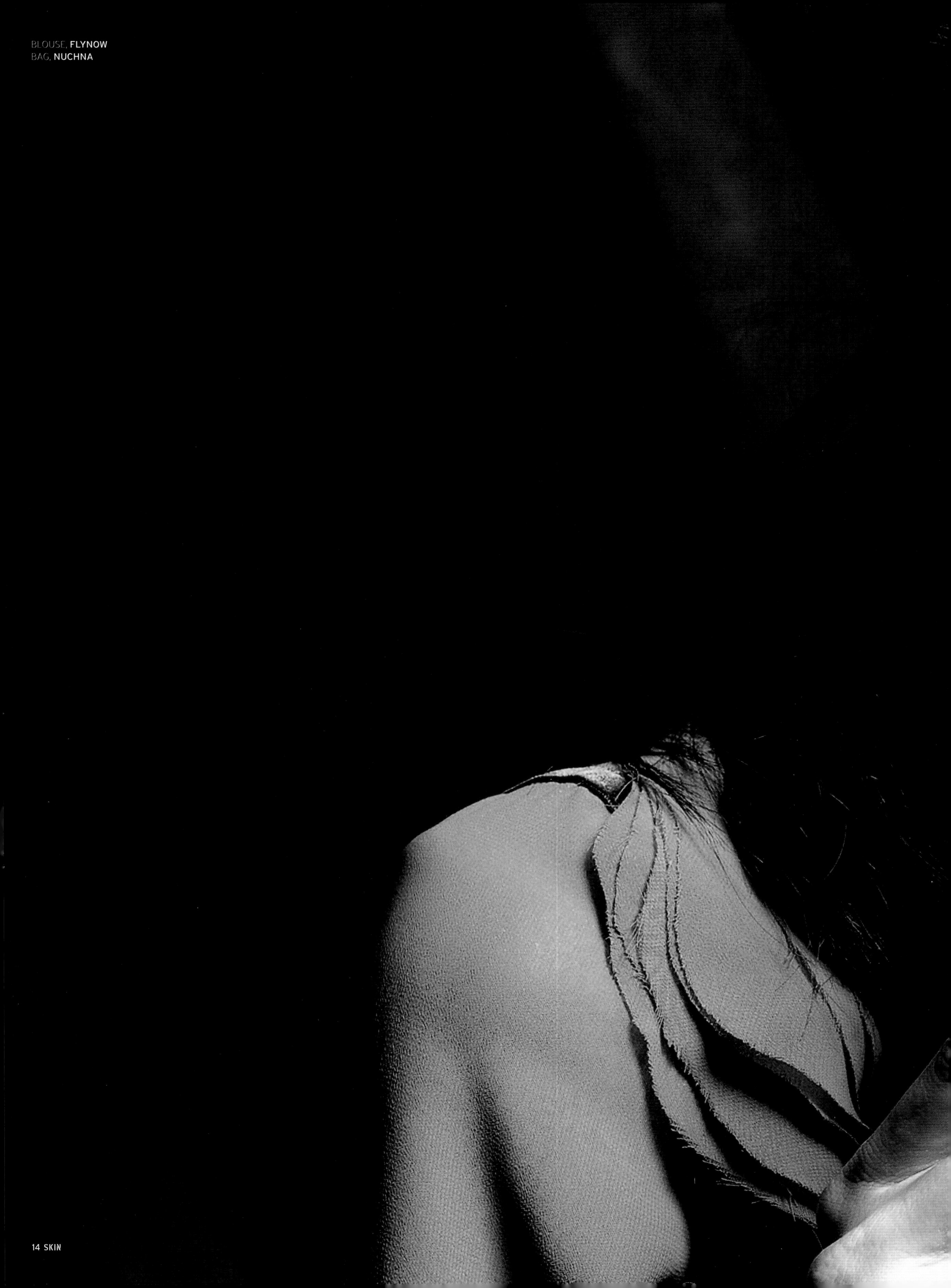

JACKET, **SUNSHINE**
SKIRT + BAG, **FLYNOW**
SHOES, **GREY**
NECKLACE, **ISSUE**

JACKET, **REALISTIC SITUATION**
SKIRT, **ISSUE**
BAG, **FLYNOW**

FROM LEFT: BAG, TANGO
SILVER PUMPS, PATNASILP
LEATHER CLUTCH, NUCHNA
SHOES, SRETSIS
BOOTS, ISSUE
SLIPPERS, NUCHNA
BAG, NUCHNA
SHOES, SRETSIS
CLUTCH, JACKIE O.

T-SHIRT, **PLAYHOUND**
SKIRT, **FLYNOW**
BRACELET, **TANGO**
BAG, **NUCHNA**

T-SHIRT, ISSUE
DRESS, BOUDOIR
BELT, MISSILE
BAG, BOYY
SHOES, TANGO

TOP, **PLAYHOUND**
SKIRT + BRACES, **CHAI**
BAG, **MISSILE**

DRESS, **ISSUE**
BELTS, **FLYNOW + CHAI**
BAG, **JACKIE O.**
SHOES, **NUCHNA**

T-SHIRT, **CHAI**
DRESS, **FLYNOW**
BELT, **JACKIE O.**
SHOES + BAG, **TANGO**

ORDINARY PEOPLE BASED ON A TRUE STORY

PHOTOGRAPHY. **PUNSIRI SIRIWETCHAPUN**
STYLING. **JIRAWAT SRILUANSOI**
ASSISTANT. **PUBETT CHAISUNTORNYOTHIN**

WHEN IT COMES TO TOP-QUALITY ACCESSORIES, THE CITIZENS OF THAILAND'S CITY OF ANGELS ARE QUITE SIMPLY SPOILT FOR CHOICE. FROM GORGEOUS GEMS TO BEGUILING BELTS TO FABULOUS FOOTWEAR, THE OPTIONS ARE SEEMINGLY ENDLESS.

AND WITH AN AMAZING ARRAY OF HANDBAGS AVAILABLE, PICKING THE PERFECT BAG MAY BE THE MOST DIFFICULT DECISION OF ALL. BUT WHO'S TO SAY THAT ONLY ONE CAN EVER REALLY BE ENOUGH? AFTER ALL, WHEN BEAUTY, QUALITY AND VARIETY CONVERGE, THERE REALLY IS NO SUCH THING AS OVERDOING IT.

CLOTHES, **REALISTIC SITUATION**

BAGS, **ALBÉDO, ALBERTO, ANNEE, BONNY CLUB, BORSALINO, BOYY, BSC, DAKS, DE NALINE, ELEGANZA, GUY LAROCHE, IRIS MONTINI, JACOB, JEAN-LOUIS SCHERRER, LA SOURIRE, LOUIS FONTAINE, MARWELL, MICHEL ANGELO, NORIKO, PHENSIAM, POLO WORLD, SEA STAR, TRAMPIONI**

SHOES, **DONPHROM, F FERRANI, PATNASILP, SENSO, SIAM MOHAWK, STAR FORD**

WITH IT'S TEMPLES AND TUK TUKS, THAILAND IS OFTEN TOUTED AS AN EXOTIC ESCAPE FOR TOURISTS LOOKING TO ENJOY THE SUN AND THE SIGHTS. AND WHILE SAFFRON-ROBED MONKS AND MAJESTIC PALACES MAY INDEED BE A DELIGHT, THE MOST EXOTIC ATTRACTIONS IN THAILAND ARE OFTEN FOUND DANGLING FROM THE ARMS OF THOSE IN THE KNOW. MADE FROM THE SKIN OF STINGRAY, OSTRICH, CROCODILE OR FRESHWATER SNAKE, THESE STUNNING HANDBAGS ARE A MUST-HAVE FOR ANYONE WITH A FLAIR FOR ADVENTURE. ALL OF THE SKIN IS LOCALLY RAISED AND TANNED BEFORE BEING TOPPED OFF WITH STRIKING DESIGNS BY SOME OF THE COUNTRY'S MOST-SKILLED CRAFTSMEN.

EMPEROR TOMATO KETCHUP

PHOTOGRAPHY. NAT PRAKOBSANTISUK
STYLING.   JIRAT SUBPISANKUL

EXOTIC LEATHER NECKLACE, JACKIE O.

PATCHED STINGRAY POUFFE, LOTUS ARTS DE VIVRE
ALLIGATOR BAG, WABINO
SHOES, NUCHNA

OSTRICH BAG, WABINO
ALLIGATOR BANGLES, JACKIE O.
STINGRAY BANGLE, LOTUS ARTS DE VIVRE

LAMPSKIN BAG, NORIKO

KEEP IT
L   O   O
KEEP IT TIGHT

FASHION PHOTOGRAPHY.   SURASAK ITTIRIT
STYLING.   SARUNYA ARIYAKUL
NON-FASHION PHOTOGRAPHY.   ASA SMUDHAVANICH

S

E,

MESSANGER BAG + WRISTBAND, THE FRAGILE
BELT, PORNCHAI

IT'S HOT

AND IT'S
BANGKOK'S
BIGGEST MARKET.

IT'S
HEAVING,

BUT
JATUJAK MARKET
IS SO MUCH
MORE THAN
A STEAMY SHOPPER'S
PARADISE;

SUEDE HAT + BELT, PORNCHAI
BAG, BLUE BORINE

IT'S ALSO A HOTBED OF FASHION IN THIS TEEMING METROPOLIS.

THAT'S RIGHT, AMIDST THE FIGHTING COCKS AND CUSTOM FURNITURE, SHOPPERS CAN DELIGHT IN SOME OF THE CITY'S FINEST FASHION.

BAG + HEADBAND, ANNA
LEATHER WRISTBAND, THE FRAGILE

FROM BRAND-NAME TO NO-NAME,

THE WINDING LANES OF THIS LABYRINTH ARE
FILLED WITH ANYTHING AND EVERYTHING
NEEDED TO CREATE OR COMPLETE THAT
UNMISTAKABLE LOOK.

AND
IF YOU
CAN'T FIND
THOSE

SNAKESKIN
BOOTS

YOU'VE ALWAYS
DREAMED ABOUT,
TAKE
HEART...

AT
LEAST
YOU

CAN

BUY
THE

SNAKE.

LEATHER CASE, PERFECT COMBINATION

Minnelli

ซื้อขา...

รองเท้าแบรนด์...

รับซักกระเป๋...

รับย้อมเครื่...

รับทำเสื้อยึดอับแจ็ค

กระเป๋า

ด์เนม มือสอง

รองเท้าหนัง

งหนัง ทุกชนิด

PHOTOGRAPHY. **NAT PRAKOBSANTISUK**
STYLING. **JIRAT SUBPISANKUL**

WALK ON

THE TROPICAL HEAT OF THAILAND'S MOST-CONGESTED CITY MAY NOT SEEM LIKE THE MOST LIKELY LOCATION FOR SPORTING THIS SEASON'S LATEST LEATHER.

AND WHILE MOST OF THE MEN IN BANGKOK WOULD SWEAT AT THE MERE THOUGHT OF TAKING A MID-DAY WALK WHILE WEARING A LEATHER JACKET, BANGKOKIANS DON'T MIND TURNING UP THE HEAT WHEN IT COMES TO ACCESSORIES. SO THOSE SEEKING TO SHOW OFF A LITTLE SKIN LOOK TO LEATHER BAGS, BELTS AND SHOES –THE PERFECT PICKS FOR SPICING UP ANY MAN'S WARDROBE.

JACKET + TROUSERS, ANR
SHOES, SUNSHINE
BAG, RAGAZZE

SHIRT + TIE, ANR
JACKET, GREYHOUND
BAG, BORSALINO

TROUSERS, ZENITH
SHOES + BAG, RAGAZZE

ABOVE ME, BELOW YOU

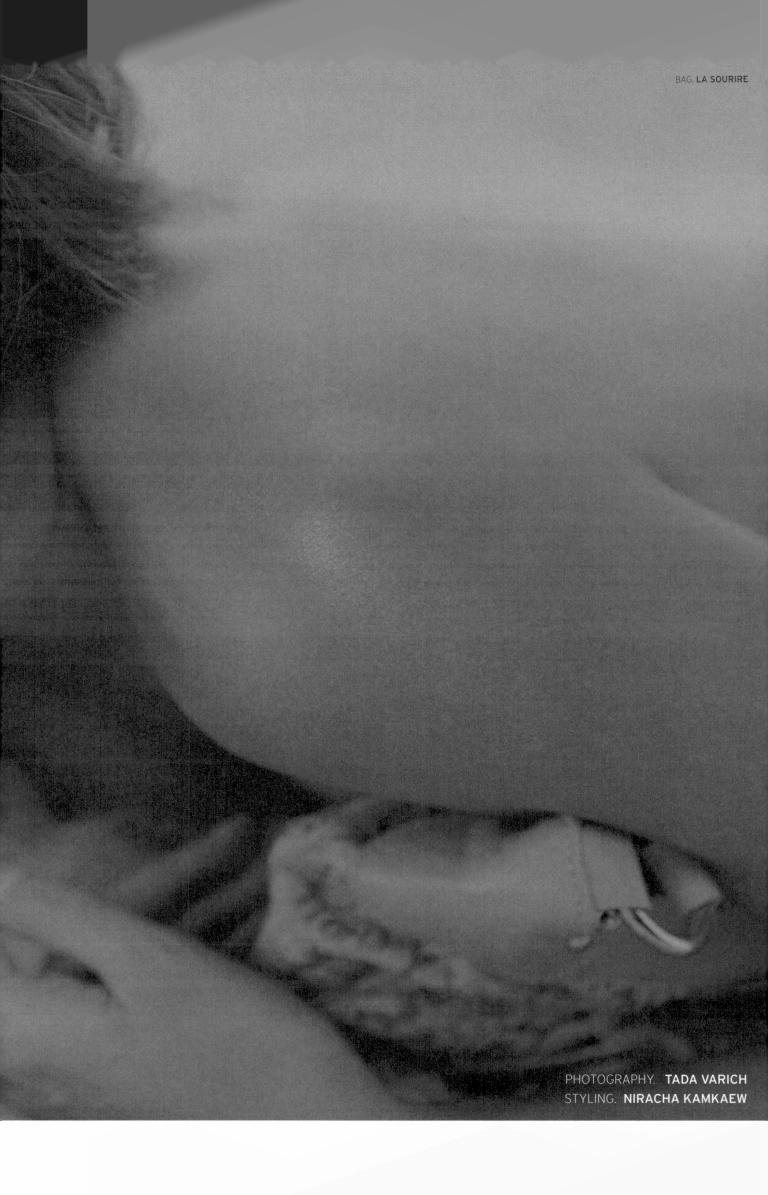

BAG, LA SOURIRE

PHOTOGRAPHY. **TADA VARICH**
STYLING. **NIRACHA KAMKAEW**

BAG, MARWELL

SKIN CAN BE SMOOTH.
SKIN CAN BE SENSUAL.
SKIN CAN BE SEXY.

AND BEAUTIFUL THAI HANDBAGS CAN BE ALL THREE
A COMBINATION OF EXCEPTIONAL DESIGN
SUPERIOR MATERIALS AND THAT LITTLE SOMETHING EXTRA,
THESE HANDBAGS ARE THE PERFECT WAY TO ADD STYLE AND
SASS TO ANY OUTFIT..
NO MATTER HOW MINIMALIST IT MAY BE

BAG, DE NALINE

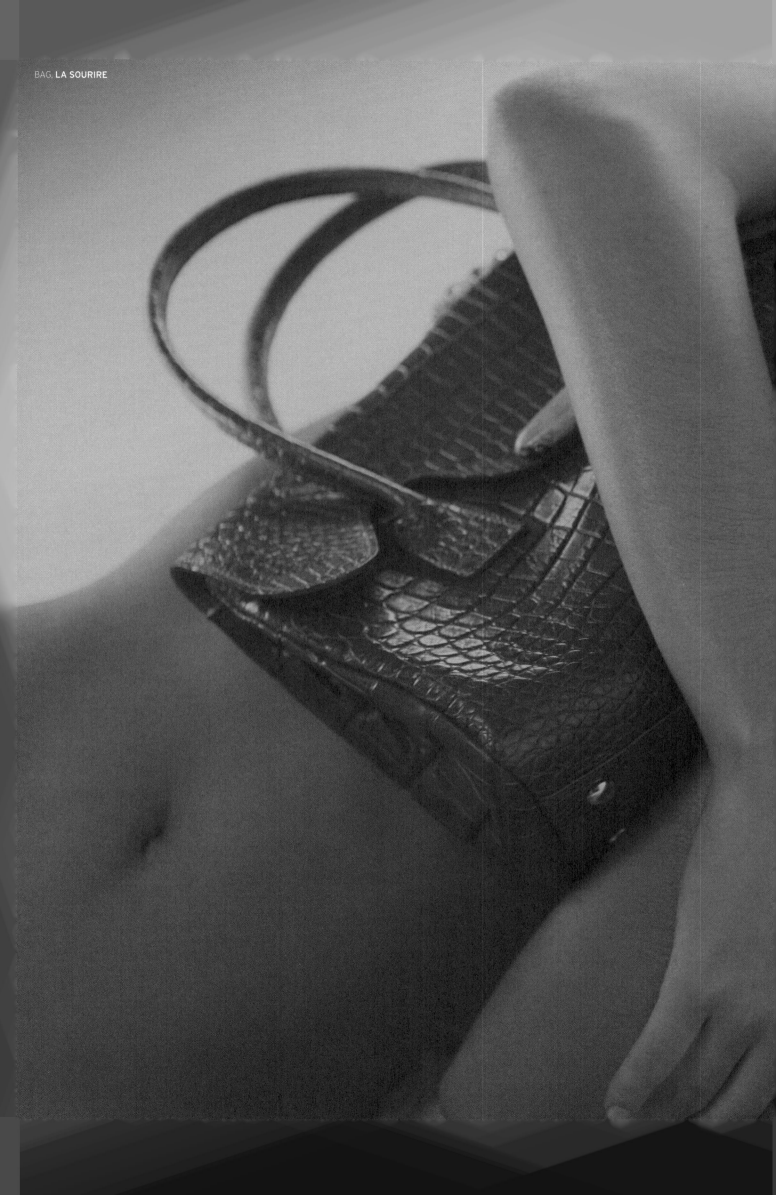

BAG, **ELEGANZA**

A

B

C

D

E

F

G

I

J

K

PROJECT CHAIRMAN
PROJECT DIRECTOR
EXECUTIVE ADVISORS

EDITOR-IN-CHIEF
EXECUTIVE EDITOR
CONTRIBUTING EDITOR

VISUAL DIRECTOR
FASHION DIRECTOR
SUB-EDITOR
EDITORIAL STAFF

WRITERS

EDITORIAL CO-ORDINATORS

CREATIVE DIRECTOR
ART DIRECTOR
DESIGNERS

PHOTOGRAPHERS

STYLISTS

STYLISTS ASSISTANT

HAIR AND MAKE-UP ARTISTS

MANAGING EDITOR
PROJECT MANAGER
PRODUCTION MANAGER
WEBSITE EDITOR

PRINT / PLATE

PRODUCER

CHAKRAMON PHASUKAVANICH
PRAMODE VIDTAYASUK
ALLAN NAMCHAISIRI
SUPREEYA SUTHAMTARIKUL
WITOON SIMACHOKEDEE

KULLAWIT LAOSUKSRI
WATCHARIN PHONGSAI
TIM LIM

NAT PRAKOBSANTISUK
JIRAT SUBPISANKUL
CHRIS BLAKE
MANIT MANEEPHANTAKUN
SUWANNEE REUNGVITAYACHOTE
CHRIS BLAKE
SAVINEE BURANASILAPIN
TOM DENNECKER
SIRIPORN MUANGWAN

PRATARN TEERATADA
PIYAPONG BHUMICHITRA
PINIDA CHAIKUL
WIWAN WORASIRI

ASA SMUDHAVANICH
NAT PRAKOBSANTISUK
PUNSIRI SIRIWETCHAPUN
SURASAK ITTIRIT
TADA VARICH

JIRAT SUBPISANKUL
JIRAWAT SRILUANSOI
NIRACHA KAMKAEW
SARUNYA ARIYAKUL
PUBETT CHAISUNTORNYOTHIN

APICHART NORASETHAPORN
NICHAKAN SUNGWIAN
O-LEK
PHORNPHAN CHANCHOLSAMUT
PUNWISIT SUKAROM
SARAWUT REKALILIT
SOMPORN TIRIN
SORAVUDH CHATRAKUL NA AYUDHAYA
SURAT YINGSOMBUT
VASANA O-ADISAI

ROCHANA KOSIYANON
CHAMAIPORN NA RANONG
ZONGZAK JITTRONG
NIRUT KRUSUANSOMBAT

SIRIVATANA INTERPRINT PUBLIC CO., LTD.

ON THE BEHALF OF
BANGKOK FASHION CITY
WWW.BANGKOKFASHIONCITY.COM
THE MINISTRY OF INDUSTRY

TTIS CO., LTD.
5TH FL. ATTHAKRAVI BLDG.
98 SUKHUMVIT 26,
KLONG TEOY, BANGKOK 10110, THAILAND
T. 662 661 2442
F. 662 661 2439
E. INFO@TTIS.CO.TH